Depression

Perspectives on Mental Health

by Judith Peacock

Consultant:
Jackie Casey, JD
Executive Director
Suicide Awareness\Voices of Education (SA\VE)

LifeMatters
an imprint of Capstone Press
Mankato, Minnesota

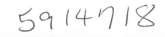

LifeMatters Books are published by Capstone Press
PO Box 669 • 151 Good Counsel Drive • Mankato, Minnesota 56002
http://www.capstone-press.com

Printed in the United States of America

Library of Congress Cataloging-in-Publication Data
Peacock, Judith, 1942-
     Depression / by Judith Peacock
          p.   cm.   (Perspectives on mental health)
     Includes bibliographical references and index.
     Summary: Defines depression and offers strategies for teens to cope with their own depression or that of others.
     ISBN 0-7368-0435-8 (lib. bdg.) — ISBN 0-7368-0440-4 (series)
     1. Depression, Mental—Juvenile literature. [1. Depression, Mental.] I. Title. II. Series.
     RC537 .P42 2000
     616.85'27—dc21   99-048411
                                               CIP

Staff Credits
Anita Larsen and Marta Fahrenz, editors; Adam Lazar, designer; Mary Donnelly, photo researcher

Photo Credits
Cover: ©Capstone Press/Adam Lazar
FPG International/©Paul Ambrose, 50
International Stock/©Scott Barrow, 27, 40; ©Patrick Ransey, 35; ©Peter Russell Clemens, 37; ©Bob Jacobson, 51
©James L. Shaffer, 10, 56
Unicorn Stock Photos/©Martin Jones, 6; ©Eric R. Berndt, 7; ©Steve Bourgeois, 29; ©Aneal Vohra, 31, 48
Uniphoto/©Llewellyn, 13; ©Peter Beck, 18; ©Bob Daemmrich, 30
Visuals Unlimited/©Terry Gleason, 45; ©Jeff Greenberg, 58

A 0 9 8 7 6 5 4 3 2 1

Table of Contents

Chapter Overview

Depression is a mood disorder. Its main symptom is a feeling of extreme sadness and hopelessness.

Depression that is not treated can affect a person's ability to function in daily life. It even may lead a person to suicide.

Several factors may contribute to depression. Changes in brain chemicals, inherited tendencies, and personality each may play a role. Other contributing factors can be a severe emotional shock, too much stress, illness, and substance use.

Anyone can have depression, even children and teens. Depression affects millions of people.

Depression is a treatable medical illness like cancer and heart disease. Nevertheless, many false ideas about depression and other mental illnesses persist.

Chapter 1

What Is Depression?

Kaleb is worried about his mother. She used to laugh and tell jokes. Now she rarely smiles and is always quiet and sad.

KALEB, AGE 15

Kaleb's mother drags herself home from work in the evening. She makes dinner for Kaleb. Then she goes to her room and shuts the door. Sometimes Kaleb hears her cry. He wishes his mother would be her old self. "What's wrong with her?" he wonders. "Why can't she just snap out of it?"

Kaleb's mother shows signs of depression. Depression is a medical illness like heart disease or cancer. It can be diagnosed, or identified, and treated. If it is not treated, however, it can have serious consequences.

A Mood Disorder

Depression affects a person's mood, or feelings. People with depression have an overwhelming feeling of sadness. They feel empty, helpless, and alone. They may not even know why they are sad.

Depression is more than having the blues. Everyone feels down and discouraged from time to time. You may feel depressed when you're sick or have a problem at school. You may be in a low mood when you fail to reach your goals. The blues usually go away in a few days.

Depression that is more than the blues is called clinical depression. It goes on for a long time and requires treatment from professionals. In this book, the word *depression* means clinical depression.

Effects of Depression

Depression affects a person's thoughts and behavior. A person with depression may have low self-esteem. He or she may feel worthless. The person may spend time worrying about real or imagined problems. People with depression often lack energy and are unable to enjoy normal pleasures.

Sleeping problems are common with depression. Some people with depression have a hard time getting to sleep. Others may fall asleep easily, but then wake up too early in the morning. They may not be able to go back to sleep. Others may sleep too much. People with depression also may lose their appetite and not want to eat. Others may eat all the time to try to feel better.

Depression can interfere with a person's ability to function in daily life. He or she may be unable to concentrate on school or other responsibilities. The depression may be so severe that the person cannot get out of bed. He or she may not even be able to get dressed.

A constant feeling of hopelessness may lead to thoughts of death. People with depression may see taking their life as the only way to end their emotional pain. Untreated depression is the most common risk factor for suicide.

Your brain can be exposed to disease and injury like any other organ in your body. One person described her depression as a "brain sprain."

Causes of Depression

No one can say for sure what causes depression to develop in a person. For some people, a combination of things may be to blame. For other people, one factor seems most significant. For still other people, depression develops for no apparent reason. Some causes or triggers of depression include changes in brain chemicals. Other causes may be inherited tendencies, emotional shock, stress, illness, or substance use.

Changes in Brain Chemicals

Depression may relate to changes in brain chemicals. Research shows that there may be a biochemical basis for depression. Its cause may be related to chemical reactions and processes in a person's body. Medical researchers have found that the brain of many depressed people has a shortage of some chemicals. Two of these are serotonin and norepinephrine, chemicals that affect a person's mood. Certain medications are known to restore the brain's chemical balance. It is not known, however, what causes the chemical imbalance. That may be due to heredity, stress, or something else.

Inherited Tendencies

Depression often occurs among members of the same family. A grandparent, parent, brother, aunt, and cousin all may have the disorder. This suggests that some people may inherit a tendency toward depression. However, depression also occurs in individuals with no family history of the illness.

Even infants who are neglected or lose their mother can develop a certain type of depression. It is called anaclitic depression.

DID YOU KNOW?

Emotional Shock

An upsetting shock, such as the death of a loved one, a divorce, or an accident, is a trauma. It is normal to feel intense sadness in these situations. After a while, however, the grief usually subsides. If it does not, the grief may have turned into depression. Grief and depression are not the same thing.

Stress

Too much daily stress can lead to depression. Stress can come from many sources. Pressures related to earning a living or caring for a family create stress for many adults. Being poor or alone can bring worry and anxiety. Some people can handle a great deal of stress. Others cannot. Stress may trigger depression more easily in people who have an inherited tendency toward depression.

Illness

The stress of coping with a serious physical illness such as diabetes or epilepsy can trigger depression. Sometimes depression develops in people with a chronic, or long-term, condition because of the way other people treat them. For example, other people may not understand the illness and may be afraid of it. They may avoid the ill person or treat him or her badly.

Lee has epilepsy, a seizure disorder. Lee sometimes has seizures at school. He falls to the floor and his body jerks all over. Many of Lee's classmates do not understand. They wrongly believe that they can catch epilepsy from Lee, so they avoid him. Other students think Lee is crazy and tease him.

LEE, AGE 13

As a result, Lee is often lonely and unhappy. He hates going to school and sometimes wishes he would die during a seizure.

Substance Use

Alcohol and other drugs can depress a person's mood. Prolonged use can lead to serious depression. Depression also can be a side effect of over-the-counter and prescription drugs. For example, depression can be a side effect of some types of blood pressure medicine.

Some people with depression use drugs or alcohol as a way to feel better. However, when the effects of the substance wear off, the depression remains.

Who Gets Depression?

Depression can happen to anyone—male or female, rich or poor. Depression can develop in people of all races. Every year, 17 million people in the United States have some type of depressive illness.

The chance is 25 percent that children who have a parent with depression will become depressed. The risk rises to 75 percent if both parents have depression. Children also may adopt the depressed parent's behavior. They may think that being sad is normal.

Depression also can occur in children and teens. Studies indicate that one in every 33 children may have depression. The rate of depression among teens may be as high as one in eight. Half of all adults with depression report that their illness began before age 20.

The Happiest Years of Your Life?

Until as late as the 1980s, most doctors did not recognize depression as a disorder in children and teens. They did not believe children and teens were mature enough emotionally to have depression. This thinking has changed. Medical experts now know that children and teens have complex emotions, just as adults do.

Many parents and other adults have a hard time believing these findings. Aren't teens supposed to be happy and carefree? What do teens have to worry about? Adults tend to forget about their own anxieties as a teen. They may remember only the good times.

The truth is that the teen years can be difficult. Just the normal process of growing up produces many stresses. Teens must adapt to a changing body, take on new responsibilities, and form new relationships. They must begin to separate from home and make their own decisions. This can be overwhelming.

In addition, today's teens must cope with different stresses than teens in the past had. Many teens now must cope with parents' divorce. Now teens must deal with the pressure not only to have sex, but also to experiment with drugs. TV and magazine ads pressure teens to look and dress a certain way. A culture of violence, crime, and gangs surrounds today's teens. At the same time, some teens may get little or no guidance from their family. Such pressures and stresses put teens at risk for depression.

Laurie is a high school senior. She is pretty, smart, and talented.

LAURIE, AGE 17

She has a steady boyfriend and a loving family. Laurie seems to have everything. She also has depression. Laurie's friends and family look at her and wonder, "What does she have to be depressed about?"

Overcoming Shame

Laurie's story illustrates a common reaction to depression. Many people may have false ideas about depression. They may not understand that depression happens to individuals just as cancer or heart disease does. They may believe that a person with depression can just snap out of it. People with depression, however, need medical treatment just as they would for other diseases.

People with depression must deal with emotional pain. They also must cope with the stigma, or mark, of shame for having a mental illness. Some people think that depression is something to be ashamed of. This old idea is wrong. People with depression are not bad, crazy, or weak. They simply are ill. They need compassion, understanding, and acceptance.

Points to Consider

What did you know about depression before reading this chapter?

What do you think of when you hear the term *mental illness*?

How would you react if someone in your family had depression?

Describe a time when you felt down in the dumps or bummed out. What would your life be like if you felt that way all the time?

Chapter Overview

Major depressive disorder is a type of mood disorder. It occurs in episodes that vary in intensity and length.

Twice as many females as males have major depression, although many males who have depression may hide it.

Major depression may occur along with physical illness, other mental disorders, and substance abuse.

Seasonal affective disorder, or SAD, is a type of major depression. Episodes of SAD correspond to the seasons.

Bipolar disorder, sometimes called manic depression, is a mood disorder characterized by extreme mood swings. It may develop in some people with major depression.

Minor depressive disorder, or dysthymia, is milder than major depression. However, it lasts longer. It may precede a major depressive episode if it is not treated.

Chapter 2

Two broad categories of mood disorders are major depressive disorder and bipolar disorder. This book focuses on major depressive disorder and the milder minor depressive disorder called dysthymia. It briefly discusses bipolar disorder.

Major Depressive Disorder

A person with major depressive disorder, or major depression, needs prompt medical attention. Major depressive disorder has some notable features. The disorder is episodic, more females than males have it, and it may co-occur with other diseases.

An Episodic Illness

Major depression is episodic, meaning that the depression comes and goes. An episode may last from two weeks up to a year. The depression gradually lifts and goes away on its own. A stressful event often triggers an episode of major depression.

Some people have only a single episode of depression in their lifetime. Other people have recurring, or returning, episodes. Many years might pass between episodes, or episodes might occur frequently.

An episode of major depression might be mild, moderate, or severe. Between episodes the person may have no symptoms or reduced symptoms. A person with severe depression might have hallucinations. The person may hear or see something that is not there. Up to 15 percent of people with severe major depression die by suicide.

CHAN, AGE 17

Doctors have told Chan's uncle and cousin that they have clinical depression. Chan's first episode of depression occurred when she and her longtime boyfriend broke up. The breakup came as a complete surprise to Chan. The two had planned to go to the prom together. Chan was shocked.

Afterward, Chan stayed in her room with the shades pulled down. She listened to sad music and cried. She didn't want to eat or to see any of her friends. She barely took care of herself. "What's the point?" she thought. "My life is over."

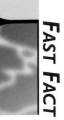

More Females Than Males

Twice as many adolescent and adult females have major depression than do males. The reasons for this are unclear. Some of the reasons may include social roles, responsibilities, the reproductive cycle, and victimization.

1. Social roles

Girls and women generally are expected to be pleasant and act "ladylike." This includes hiding their anger. When anger is constantly kept inside, it can lead to depression.

2. Responsibilities

Many women have the major responsibility for raising children or caring for aging parents. Most likely they also are employed full time. Having so many responsibilities raises the level of stress for these women.

3. Reproductive cycle

Menstruation, pregnancy, and menopause can bring changes in mood. Menstruation occurs each month when the uterus, the female organ that holds a baby before birth, sheds its lining. Menopause is when menstruation stops permanently. For some women, these physical changes also may produce depression.

4. Victimization

Women are more likely than men to be victims of physical and sexual abuse. People who feel they have little or no control over their life often become depressed.

A boy in Nicole's math class has been bothering her for the past several weeks. He calls her dirty names and says he wants to have sex with her. He touches her breasts and tries to grab her crotch. Nicole talked with her math teacher, who moved the boy to a seat across the room. That didn't help. The boy still bothers Nicole in the hallways and on the bus.

Nicole now dreads going to school. She can't concentrate on her schoolwork, and her grades are dropping. Nicole's stomach is upset all the time, and she's tired and irritable. Nothing seems fun anymore.

Some experts believe that more males may have depression than are diagnosed with it. Social roles and expectations may discourage males from seeking help for depression. Adolescent boys may hide feelings of depression because they fear others will think they are weak or not in control. These fears can prevent them from getting the help they need.

Co-occurring Illnesses

Major depression develops in many people with other illnesses such as diabetes, heart disease, cancer, and stroke. Doctors have more difficulty treating illnesses that co-occur with depression. The person's chances of recovery from the illness also are reduced.

Other mental disorders can co-occur with major depression. Two of these are the eating disorders anorexia nervosa and bulimia. These disorders particularly affect teen girls. Other disorders, such as attention deficit hyperactivity disorder (ADHD), occur in 50 percent of children or teens with depression. ADHD is a learning and behavioral disorder in which the person has difficulty concentrating and may act impulsively.

Many people who are addicted to alcohol and other drugs also are depressed. They may have turned to alcohol and drugs to deaden their emotional pain.

Depression that co-occurs with a physical illness, other mental disorder, or substance abuse may not be recognized. Both illnesses require treatment.

Seasonal Affective Disorder
Seasonal affective disorder, or SAD, is a type of major depression. Its episodes correspond to the seasons. SAD begins in the fall when daylight decreases. It improves in the spring when days get longer. People with SAD may feel slow, anxious, and irritable during the dark winter months.

Phototherapy can help lift the mood of these people. This treatment involves sitting under special lights 30 or more minutes each morning and evening. Some people with SAD move to areas with more hours of daylight during the winter.

Bipolar Disorder

People with bipolar disorder have extreme mood swings. They alternate between feeling very high (mania) and feeling very low (depression). (Bipolar disorder formerly was called manic depression.) In between extremes, these people generally have periods of normal moods.

Bipolar disorder can be distressing and disruptive. During the manic phase, the person may act recklessly. He or she may go on a wild spending spree or make foolish decisions. The person may go for days without sleeping.

Bipolar disorder affects males and females equally. It usually begins in adolescence or young adulthood and continues throughout life. Some people who experience a single episode of major depression subsequently will have a manic episode.

Minor Depressive Disorder

Minor depressive disorder, or dysthymia, is similar to major depression. The symptoms of dysthymia are milder and longer lasting than those of major depression. Instead of being episodic, the symptoms can continue for many years. The symptoms may seem to be part of the person's personality. People with dysthymia are able to function in daily life. However, they do not seem to enjoy living.

"I was on the verge of tears all the time, and I didn't know why. I felt like I had fallen into a black hole and couldn't get out. When I looked in the mirror, I didn't recognize the thin, hollow-eyed girl staring back."
—Mikayla, age 16

Dysthymia usually starts in adolescence or young adulthood. Many people with untreated dysthymia go on to have a major depressive episode.

FLORIN, AGE 16

Florin is a quiet, slow-moving guy. Some people might even say he's dull. Florin never seems too happy or excited about anything. He spends a lot of time playing video games by himself. Florin's parents sometimes feel the urge to light a fire under him. Then they shrug and think, "That's just the way Florin is." Florin's parents do not know that their son actually has dysthymia.

Points to Consider

Do you know anyone who seems down all the time? How do you react to that person?

How might having major depression affect your daily life?

Why might depression develop in people with a serious physical illness?

Chapter
Overview

People with depression need the help of mental health professionals to feel better.

Recognizing the symptoms of depression is the first step toward getting help.

Depressed teens may show their depression in angry, rebellious behavior.

Teens who think they may be depressed or know someone who may be depressed should talk with a trusted adult. This person can put them in contact with mental health professionals.

Crisis hot lines are available to help depressed persons who feel suicidal. Many organizations exist to help people with depression and their families.

Chapter 3

Depression is a real illness. People with heart disease and cancer cannot cure themselves. In the same way, people with depression cannot cure themselves. They need the help of mental health professionals and other concerned individuals.

Symptoms of Depression

Have you ever wondered if you or someone you know was seriously depressed? Only a trained professional such as a psychiatrist or a psychologist can tell for sure. However, knowing the symptoms of depression can be the first step in getting help. The following checklist is based on one developed by the National Mental Health Association.

Are You Depressed?

Read the statements below. Circle the answer next to each statement that applies to you.

YES	NO	A persistent sad, anxious, or "empty" mood, or excessive crying
YES	NO	Reduced appetite and weight loss or increased appetite and weight gain
YES	NO	Persistent physical symptoms that do not respond to treatment, such as headaches, digestive disorders, and chronic pain
YES	NO	Irritability
YES	NO	Restlessness
YES	NO	Decreased energy, fatigue, feeling "slowed down"
YES	NO	Feelings of guilt, worthlessness, helplessness, hopelessness, and gloom
YES	NO	Sleeping too much or too little, early-morning waking
YES	NO	Loss of interest or pleasure in activities once enjoyed
YES	NO	Difficulty concentrating, remembering, or making decisions
YES	NO	Thoughts of death or suicide, or suicide attempts

How did you score? A person who has five or more of these symptoms for longer than two weeks may be depressed.

You can call **1-800-573-4433** for the location of places near you that conduct screening tests for depression. The National Mental Illness Screening Project operates this service.

Symptoms of Depression in Teens

The symptoms in the checklist describe adults with depression. They also fit most depressed teens and children. However, they do not fit all depressed teens, especially males.

Instead of being sad and withdrawn, some teens act out their depression. They become angry and hostile. They may get into fights or other trouble at home and school. They may begin using alcohol and other drugs. Some depressed teens run away from home.

Examples of other ways teens might show depression are:

Being constantly bored and lacking interest in any activity

Taking unnecessary risks

Getting poor grades in school

Hurting themselves and making it seem like an accident

Beginning or increasing sexual activity

Getting into trouble with the law because of shoplifting, damaging property, and so on

Depressed teens who are angry may not get the help they need. Adults may view these teens as troublemakers and lack sympathy for them. These teens may be either avoided or punished.

If You Need Help

If you think you might be depressed, you need to talk with a trusted adult right away. Sharing your feelings with a friend your age can help. However, adults usually are better able to help you find the resources you need to get better.

Many adults are available to help you. If possible, talk with your parents about your feelings. You may think that your parents are too busy to listen or that they won't understand. Give your parents a chance to hear what you're going through. Chances are they will understand and do all they can to help.

If talking with your parents isn't possible, you might talk with another adult. A teacher, coach, or school guidance counselor can help. A family doctor or a religious leader also can help. Your community may have a walk-in counseling center for teens.

Keep telling someone until you get the help you need. Not all adults understand depression. Use this book to help educate them.

Alana felt bad and didn't know why. One day her soccer coach said, "Alana, I haven't seen you smile for a long time. Is there anything wrong?" Alana was embarrassed that her coach had noticed. Her lip quivered, and tears welled up in her eyes. Before she knew it, she was crying uncontrollably. The coach let Alana cry. Then they talked.

The coach said Alana might be depressed. She said she would ask Alana's parents to make an appointment for Alana to see a psychologist. Alana felt the dark cloud she was under lift a little. She was glad she had finally confided in someone who could help.

If Someone You Know Needs Help

Perhaps you think a family member or friend may be depressed. You can encourage that person to seek treatment. Depressed people often need encouragement to get help. They may be too confused and withdrawn to recognize their situation. They may lack the motivation and energy to seek help.

Communication is key to helping a depressed person. Describe the symptoms you see and give examples. Suggest that these are symptoms of depression. Let the person know that help is available. Be ready to listen.

Up to 15 percent of U.S. public schools now have mental health programs to help students deal with emotional problems. Such programs typically feature a mental health counselor. The counselor's main role is to listen to students' concerns. Schools with mental health programs report that grades and attendance are up and discipline problems are down. What's more, students learn that it is okay to go to counseling.

Your friend or family member may become angry. If that happens, ask a trusted adult to talk with the person. You will not be revealing a secret. You are helping someone to feel better. You even may save the person's life.

When you talk with someone who is depressed, it is important to honor the person's feelings. Saying the wrong things may make the person feel guilty. It even may make the person feel more helpless. Here are some examples of how to turn hurtful comments into helpful ones:

Hurtful	Helpful
"Let's go see a funny movie. You'll forget your problems."	"Let's go for a walk. We haven't talked in a long time."
"Just be glad you don't live in some war-torn country. Think of how lucky you are."	"You look sad. Anything bothering you?"
"Things can't be that bad."	"Can I help? I'd like to listen if you want to talk."
"You're just going through a stage. You'll get over it."	"I'm worried about you."
"I can't believe you think that way."	"Help me understand what you're feeling."

Ryan's high school held an assembly on mental health. A

psychologist described the symptoms of depression. A woman told about her son's experience with the illness. Ryan began to wonder if depression was the cause of his brother's behavior. His brother, Rocky, was 14 and in junior high. He seemed pretty messed up after their parents' divorce. Rocky had started hanging out with drug users and skipping school.

Ryan told his mother about the assembly. He showed her a pamphlet about depression. Ryan's mother said she thought Rocky would straighten himself out. So Ryan went to his father. His dad made an appointment for Rocky to see a mental health counselor.

Help in a Crisis

If you or someone you know feels suicidal, get help immediately. You might call a crisis or suicide hot line. These numbers usually are listed at the front of the telephone book under emergency numbers. You also can look under *Suicide Intervention* in the directory. Calling the police or a hospital are other good choices.

Trained volunteers staff crisis hot lines. They know how to listen to people in distress. They know how to direct callers to people and places for help. If a caller is threatening suicide, crisis-center workers can help the person think more clearly. Crisis hot line counselors answer the phone 24 hours a day. The national number **1-800-SUICIDE** is connected to local sites in many cities.

You Are Not Alone

There's another way that teens can start getting help for themselves or someone else. That is to learn all they can about depression. The back of this book lists helpful books and organizations to contact for information about depression. People with depression do not need to suffer alone. A great deal of help is available.

Do you know anyone who shows symptoms of depression?
How could you help that person to seek treatment?

If you felt you were depressed, what adult would you tell?
Why would you choose that person?

What is your school doing to tell students about depression?

Chapter Overview

Only trained health professionals are equipped to diagnose depression.

The diagnostic process includes a physical exam, medical history, interviews, and psychological testing. The mental health professional uses this information to make a diagnosis and recommendation.

Although depression is treatable, only one-third of depressed persons ever seek diagnosis and treatment.

Untreated depression can be costly in both human suffering and dollars.

Teens with untreated depression often become depressed adults.

Chapter **4**

How Is Depression Diagnosed?

Depression can be difficult to diagnose, or identify. It is especially hard to diagnose in children and teens. The symptoms vary widely among these age groups. In addition, teens are going through many changes that affect mood and behavior. Telling the difference between normal teen mood swings and major depression takes an expert.

The American Medical Association recommends that schools routinely screen at-risk students for depression. At-risk students are those who:

Show a drop in grades

Have problems in their family

Abuse alcohol or other drugs

Report physical or sexual abuse

Have issues with sexual or gender orientation

Who Can Diagnose Depression?

Various mental health professionals have the training to diagnose and treat depression. Such professionals include:

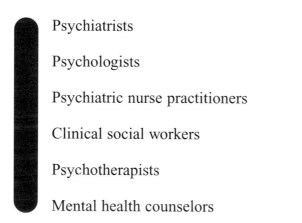

Psychiatrists

Psychologists

Psychiatric nurse practitioners

Clinical social workers

Psychotherapists

Mental health counselors

Psychiatrists also are medical doctors. Of all the mental health professionals, only psychiatrists can prescribe medications for depression. General physicians such as a family doctor can prescribe medications as well.

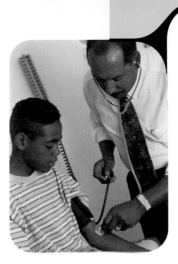

Steps in Diagnosis

Determining depression is a three-step process. It includes an interview, testing, and diagnosis and recommendation. At the beginning of the process, the mental health professional—typically a psychologist—might recommend a physical examination. The professional will want to rule out a physical illness as the cause of depressive symptoms. For example, trouble sleeping and lack of energy occur in diabetes, cancer, and other illnesses.

The psychologist strives to establish a feeling of ease and goodwill, or rapport, with the patient. This includes making the person feel comfortable and safe. A person who feels relaxed and secure is more likely to open up and answer questions honestly. Establishing rapport is important in working with teens, who often hide their feelings from adults.

Interview

The first step in diagnosing depression is to interview the person. The psychologist also may talk with family members. In the case of children, the psychologist may talk with teachers as well. These people might reveal information that the depressed person is unwilling or unable to share.

One authority divides teen drug abusers into two groups. The Sensation Seekers are a majority, and the Self-Medicators are a minority. The Self-Medicators take drugs to control the symptoms of their depression. A different type of antidrug campaign is needed for these teens. Saying that drugs will "fry their brain" makes no difference to them.

The interview includes gathering information about the person's medical history. The psychologist will want to know if parents or close relatives have had depression. Information about any traumatic experiences or substance abuse can be important for diagnosis.

The interview also includes questions about the person's current situation. The psychologist will ask about home life, school or work, relationships, problems, and feelings. During the interview, the psychologist will observe the person's level of distress and general ability to function.

Testing

The second step in diagnosing depression is psychological testing. The psychologist may ask the person to complete checklists or rating scales. The person also may be asked to solve problems, interpret pictures, or answer questions. The person's responses indicate his or her thoughts and feelings. Responses also give an idea of personality and ability to cope with stress. Some psychological tests are specially designed for diagnosing depression in children and teens.

Tony's parents took him to a psychologist for a mental health evaluation. They were worried that Tony was depressed.

TONY, AGE 15

The psychologist showed Tony a drawing of a man. The man was standing on a bridge and looking into the water below. The psychologist asked Tony to make up a story to go with the picture.

"This guy is thinking about killing himself," said Tony. "Any minute now he's going to climb up on the guard rail and jump in. He thinks he's stupid and ugly. No one likes him. He'll never be missed." The psychologist showed Tony several other drawings. Tony's stories all had themes of sadness and hopelessness.

Diagnosis and Recommendation

It may take two or more sessions before the psychologist is ready to make a diagnosis. There is no sure-fire test for depression. The psychologist must make an informed judgment based on the interview and testing. Clinical experience in working with depressed persons also helps with the diagnosis.

FAST FACT

About two-thirds of young people with mental health problems do not get the help they need.

The psychologist will call a conference to go over the results of testing and explain the diagnosis. He or she will recommend a course of treatment. It is up to the person and the person's family to follow through on the recommendation. The family may want to get a second opinion.

A Vicious Circle

Depression is a treatable medical illness. More than 80 percent of people with depression can be treated successfully. Even those with severe major depression can be helped. Unfortunately, only one in three depressed persons ever seeks diagnosis and treatment. Some reasons for this low rate include lack of information, shame, and the cost of treatment.

Lack of Information

Many people do not know the symptoms of depression. Depression often disguises itself as a physical ailment like ulcers, backache, or stomachache. People may go to the doctor for treatment of these symptoms and not mention their depressed feelings. As a result, depression can go undiagnosed or be misdiagnosed. Fortunately, more doctors now ask their patients about depression.

Many people do not know about treatments for depression. If they did, they would know that there are ways to beat depression. Believing that depression is incurable leads to more feelings of hopelessness. Finally, people with depression may not want to burden their family. Depressed teens may feel they are letting their parents down. They may feel ashamed of their behavior. Shame adds to their depression.

Shame

Depressed people often are reluctant to admit their illness. They may believe that having depression is a sign of weakness or failure. Teens in particular may deny their depression. Most teens want desperately to fit in. They may see depression as making them different, weird, or crazy.

In fact, depression is nothing to be ashamed of. Getting help for depression can change a teen's life for the better.

Cost of Treatment

Some people do not seek treatment for depression because they cannot afford it. They may lack health insurance or their insurance may not cover the cost of treating mental illness. They may not realize how costly untreated depression can be.

The Costs of Untreated Depression

People with depression may choose to tough it out. They wait for the depression to subside. In the meantime, their life is miserable. They may do serious harm to themselves while depressed.

Undiagnosed and untreated depression is especially tragic for teens. The teen years are a time for social, intellectual, and emotional growth. Depressed teens may miss out on important steps that prepare them to be adults. These teens may start down a wrong path, such as drug or alcohol abuse. This path can lead to a lifetime of hardship and unhappiness.

Depression is costly in other ways, too. People with depression lose money in wages and salary when they are unable to work. Companies lose money when depressed employees are not productive.

Rita is a teen with undiagnosed depression. She uses drugs to make herself feel better. She began to steal money from her parents to pay for her habit. They found out and threw her out of the house. Now Rita lives on the streets with other homeless kids. She supports her drug addiction through various illegal activities. A counselor at a shelter for runaways persuaded Rita to have a blood test. She tested positive for human immunodeficiency virus (HIV), a sexually transmitted disease.

Points to Consider

Is there a history of depression in your family?

If you were depressed, would you seek treatment? Why or why not?

What could be done to encourage more people with depression to seek treatment?

Do you think it is a good idea for schools to identify at-risk students and screen them for depression? Why or why not?

Chapter Overview

With proper treatment, most people with depression can return to normal daily activities within a few weeks.

Antidepressants and psychotherapy are the main treatments for depression. Antidepressants are drugs that help to relieve depression. The person is able to function more normally.

Psychotherapy means talking with a trained therapist about depression-related problems. The person learns to change negative patterns of thinking, feeling, and acting.

Hospitalization may be required if the person is at risk for suicide or is withdrawing from alcohol or drugs.

People with milder forms of depression might use alternative therapies to lift their mood.

Chapter **5**

How Is Depression Treated?

Mental health professionals treat depression with medication or psychotherapy. They often use a combination of the two. The type of treatment depends on the severity of the depression. As with any illness, the sooner treatment begins, the better the chances for success.

Antidepressants

Medications for depression are called antidepressants. Their purpose is to restore depressed people to a normal mood. Antidepressants do not make people extremely happy or the world rosy. People who take antidepressants still may need to work on self-esteem, social skills, and other problems. The medication makes their emotions stable so they can cope with daily life.

Antidepressants may take from four to eight weeks to help a depressed person feel better. A period of trial and error may be necessary to find the right antidepressant.

Some people need to take antidepressants for a short time before their symptoms improve or disappear. Other people need to take antidepressants for the rest of their life. Antidepressants are not habit forming. They work only for people who need them. Antidepressants do not change a person's personality. Instead, they let the person's true personality emerge.

Types of Antidepressants

Antidepressants increase the levels of the brain chemicals that regulate emotions. Two important chemicals are serotonin and norepinephrine. Four main types of antidepressants each work on brain chemicals in different ways.

1. **Selective serotonin reuptake inhibitors (SSRIs).** Well-known antidepressants such as Prozac®, Zoloft®, and Paxil® belong to this group.

2. **Tricyclic antidepressants (TCAs).** These are an older type of antidepressant.

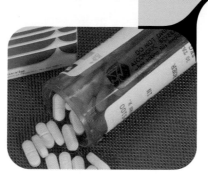

3. **Monoamine oxidase inhibitors (MAOIs).** These antidepressants can cause dangerous interactions with certain foods and other drugs. They are seldom recommended for children and teens.

4. **Serotonin/norepinephrine reuptake inhibitors (SNRIs).** SNRIs and SSRIs tend to have fewer side effects. They are the antidepressants most often prescribed for children and teens.

Side Effects

Antidepressants can cause side effects, especially when a person first starts taking the drugs. Side effects can include nervousness, shakiness, or nausea, the urge to throw up. Other side effects may be dry mouth, constipation, or weight gain. Some people experience blurred vision or headaches. Side effects often go away once the person's body has adjusted to the medicine.

People on antidepressants may feel worse before they start to feel better. Some people may become impatient and quit taking their medication. A smarter idea would be to talk with the doctor. He or she can help find a more effective dosage or a medication with fewer side effects.

People on antidepressants also should consult their doctor before taking any over-the-counter medications or herbal remedies. It is never a good idea to drink alcohol or use other drugs while on antidepressants. The combination could be deadly.

Treatment for depression can be expensive. Your family's health insurance might not cover the cost of antidepressants and therapy. If that is the case, you might seek help from a community mental health agency. Such agencies often provide treatment on a sliding-scale arrangement. That means people pay only what they can afford. Mental health organizations also can help families find sources of financial aid.

Teens and Antidepressants

Prescribing antidepressants for teens and children is controversial. Some mental health professionals oppose it. Their concern is that not enough is known about the long-term effects of antidepressants on developing brains and bodies. Little research has been done on the safety and effectiveness of antidepressants for children and teens. In addition, professionals worry about how easy it can be to overprescribe antidepressants. They say that therapy or alternative treatments should be tried as well.

Other mental health professionals support prescribing antidepressants for teens and children. They think it is wrong to withhold a treatment that might help. They believe antidepressants can prevent young people from turning to alcohol and other drugs for relief.

Tanya has been taking an antidepressant for three years.

Before then, she was a nervous wreck. Tanya cried at the slightest problem. She couldn't be left alone, even for a few minutes. She worried constantly that burglars were breaking into the house or that her parents were dying. She stopped eating regularly.

When therapy alone didn't help, Tanya's doctor put her on an antidepressant as well. The addition of medication gave Tanya a new life. Today she is a well-adjusted teen. She is on the honor roll at school and has many friends. Tanya and her family are grateful for antidepressants.

Psychotherapy

Psychotherapy means talk therapy. The depressed person talks with a trained therapist about his or her problems. The therapist usually is a psychiatrist or psychologist. Psychotherapy can be especially effective for less severe cases of depression. Improvement generally is seen after 10 to 20 weeks of treatment.

Types of psychotherapy differ. One type attempts to change the person's negative ways of thinking and behaving. Another focuses on improving the person's relationships with other people. Still another explores reasons for the person's depression.

Therapists may meet alone with the depressed person, or they might include the person in a group. Group therapy often works well for teens. Teens tend to discuss their problems more freely with other teens. Group members can offer each other advice and support. Family therapy also may benefit people with depression.

Therapists keep anything their clients tell them in confidence. They will not tell parents what a teen says in sessions unless the teen wants them to. Therapists usually provide a way for clients to contact them 24 hours a day.

JUSTIN, AGE 16

Justin's parents made an appointment for him to talk with a psychiatrist. At first, Justin didn't want to go. "Psychiatrists are for crazy people," he said. "I'm not crazy!"

After meeting a few times with the psychiatrist, however, Justin began to change his mind about therapy. "This guy's really cool," he thought. "He knows how to listen. He got me to talk. I feel like I can tell him anything and he won't judge me."

Justin met with his psychiatrist for several more sessions. In a few weeks, he was thinking more clearly about his problems. He was learning better ways to deal with stress and anger.

Some experts believe pet therapy can elevate the mood of people with depression. Research has shown that pet therapy helps people with depression and other illnesses feel less isolated and lonely.

Hospitalization

Most often, depression is treated without hospitalization. The person goes to the therapist's office or to a mental health center, receives treatment, and then goes home. Sometimes, however, the depressed person must be hospitalized. The person may be at risk for suicide or may be withdrawing from alcohol or other drugs. The person may need to be taken out of a stressful environment for a while. After discharge from the hospital, the person receives follow-up therapy.

Alternative Therapies

Some people with depression turn to alternative therapies. These therapies are different from traditional medicine in North America. Many therapies have ancient origins. Healers in many of these therapies are called practitioners. Patients may be called clients.

Alternative therapies may help to lower stress and increase energy. Some may work on the brain to elevate mood. Some alternative therapies are acupuncture, biofeedback, and herbs and supplements. Therapies such as herbal remedies and supplements should be used with a doctor's approval.

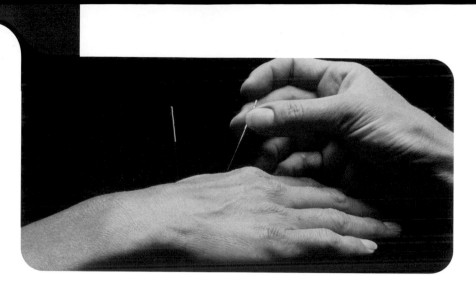

Acupuncture

Acupuncture is an ancient Chinese method of healing.
Acupuncturists insert fine needles at specific points on the body.
They seek to restore a healthy flow of life energy through a
person's body. Practitioners can be found in the phone book under
Acupuncture or *Health Services.*

Biofeedback

In biofeedback, an electronic monitor is connected to the skin.
The monitor measures heart rate, blood pressure, muscle tension,
brain wave activity, and skin temperature. A trained practitioner
interprets the information for the client. The aim is to help clients
learn how to control bodily responses with their mind.
Practitioners are listed in the phone book under headings such as
Biofeedback Therapists, Physicians/Psychiatrists, Psychologists,
or *Psychotherapists.*

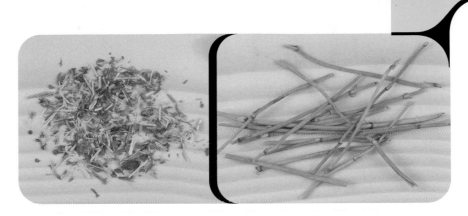

Herbal Remedies and Supplements

Medicinal herbs have been used throughout history. Some herbs are better known than others. For example, you may have seen ads for St. John's wort on TV. Doctors in Germany often prescribe this herb to treat depression. Several studies have shown St. John's wort to be effective for mild to moderate depression. Not much is known about its side effects. North American doctors do not usually prescribe it. Practitioners who offer herbal remedies can be found in the phone book under *Herbal Medicine, Chinese Medicine,* and *Naturopathy.*

SAMe, a dietary supplement similar to a vitamin, has been used to treat depression. Some studies have shown that SAMe helps mild to major depression without the side effects common to antidepressants. The supplement has been used in Europe for about 20 years. Few studies on SAMe have been done in North America.

Points to Consider

What might be some disadvantages in using antidepressants alone to treat depression in teens?

Why might teens be reluctant to get therapy for depression?

How could you help a friend or family member who is in treatment for depression?

Chapter Overview

Even though a person's depression has been treated successfully, depression can return.

People with depression need the love and support of family and friends to get and stay well. There are many things family and friends can do to help the depressed person.

People who have experienced depression can reduce the risk of having their symptoms return. Most important is to stick with their treatment plan.

Chapter **6**

Staying Well

Proper treatment can help people with depression return to normal daily activities. They soon can enjoy living again. Depression, however, can creep back into a person's life. People who have experienced depression must strive to stay well.

People recovering from depression need the love and support of family and friends. They need to know that they are not alone.

"I keep a mood chart. At the end of each day I write on my chart how I felt. When I can look back and see more good days than bad, I know I'm getting better."
—Leah, age 16

BONITA, AGE 15

Bonita's mother is undergoing treatment for depression. Bonita has mixed feelings about her mother's illness. On the one hand, Bonita loves her mother and wants to help her. On the other hand, she feels anger and resentment. Her mother's depression has caused a lot of problems for the family. Bonita has had to do more around the house. She's missed out on fun with her friends.

Bonita knows her mother has been through a lot. Even so, it is sometimes hard to be sympathetic. Bonita can't help feeling her mother could get better faster if she tried harder.

If You Know Someone With Depression

If you have a family member or friend with depression, here are eight ways you can help.

1. Encourage the person to stay in treatment.

Remind the person that with time and help, he or she may feel better. You might do things that make it easier for the person to go to treatment. You could pick up assignments and books for a friend. You could baby-sit younger siblings or do extra chores if your parent is in treatment.

2. Participate in family therapy.

Depression affects family members, too. Family members may need to learn new ways of talking and behaving around one another. Family therapy is an opportunity to get problems out in the open and work on solutions.

3. Involve the person in activities.

Invite the person to go on a walk or to a movie. At first, you might have to insist that the person get active. You also may want to limit the activity to just you and your friend or family member. Later on, when the person is up to it, you can include more people.

4. Reassure the person that you care about him or her.

Give the person a pat on the back or a hug. Send a note of encouragement.

5. Do not make the person feel guilty.

Remember that depression happens. It is no one's fault.

6. Do not do too much for the person.

The person will need to accept some responsibility for his or her daily activities. This can help restore self-worth and self-confidence.

7. Do not pressure the person to be cheerful.

Pressuring the person to be cheerful may make him or her angry. The person might feel even more helpless.

8. Do not nag the person to tell his or her thoughts.
Let the person know you are willing to listen when he or she is
ready to talk.

A Word of Warning

Family and friends may think the problem is solved when a person
who has been suicidal begins to feel better. They may think it is
safe to relax and return to their usual activities. However, the
person may be in more danger of suicide at this time than earlier.
He or she may have been too confused and tired to carry out a
suicide plan while deeply depressed. The return of energy makes
it easier for the person to take action now.

Take Care of Yourself

Living or being with a depressed person can be difficult. There
will be many hard feelings to face. You may feel impatient and
frustrated with the person. You may feel angry about the problems
the person's depression has caused. You may worry about what
will become of the person. All of these feelings are natural.

People living with a depressed person can begin to feel down
themselves. You can avoid this by taking care of yourself. Find
someone you can share your feelings with. Keep in touch with
friends and relatives. Continue doing things you enjoy.

Vigorous exercise releases endorphins. These are brain chemicals that lift mood and help a person feel energized. They're natural antidepressants.

If You Have Depression

Can depression be prevented? That's hard to answer. People may not be able to prevent getting heart disease or cancer. They can, however, do things to lower their risk of getting these diseases. For example, not smoking reduces the chances for heart attack and some forms of cancer. In the same way, you can do things to keep depression from controlling your life again. Here are some suggestions.

1. Stick with your treatment plan.

It is important to take your medication as directed. Go to therapy and join a support group. Talk with your mental health professional if problems develop with your treatment plan. The plan can be adjusted as needed. Stay with your plan even when you start feeling better. Quitting before your therapist gives the okay could be dangerous.

2. Practice good health habits.

This may sound like old news, but it is extremely important to keep your body healthy. Poor eating habits and lack of exercise may contribute to depression. Eat a balanced diet, exercise regularly, drink eight glasses of water each day, and so on. When your body feels good, your spirit will lighten up, too.

3. Be around other people.

Don't stay alone constantly. Get out and do things with other people. This may feel awkward at first, especially if you've been out of touch for a while. Take it slow. Begin by doing something with just one friend. You will need to decide what you want to tell people about your depression.

4. Keep busy, but not too busy.

Hobbies, sports, clubs, or volunteering can help build self-esteem. Keeping busy also leaves less time to worry about problems. Of course, it is important to find a balance. You don't want to be so busy that you get stressed out. You still need time just to relax.

5. Clean up messes from the past and move on.

You may have hurt others and yourself when you were depressed. For example, you may have let your grades drop. Do what you can to make things right and then move on. You might ask your teachers how you could make up poorly done or missed assignments.

6. Face your feelings and deal with them.

Learn to recognize your feelings and handle them in appropriate ways. If you're angry, write about your feelings. If you're sad, cry. If you're lonely, visit someone. Talking about painful emotions with an adult is a good release. It also lets the adult know what's going on with you.

Someday health insurance companies may pay the cost of treating mental illnesses as they do for physical illnesses. State and federal governments are working toward this goal. The Mental Health Parity Act of 1996 is a start. This bill applies only to insurance companies that already pay the cost of treating mental health illnesses. These companies must offer equal benefits for both mental health illnesses and physical illnesses.

HOLLY, AGE 15

Every so often, Holly's grandmother takes Holly to lunch at the Fairfax Tea Room. Gran asks Holly all about school, sports, and boys. One time after lunch, Gran leaned over and took Holly's hand. "Being young," she said, "isn't always the best time of your life." Holly knew then that Gran understood about being a teen. Holly feels comfortable talking with Gran about anything. She wishes all kids had such a loving, watchful adult in their life.

Points to Consider

What other suggestions can you make for coping with depression?

If you were recovering from depression, what would you say to others about your illness?

What might a depressed teen from a difficult family situation do to improve his or her situation? List three places he or she could go for help.

How could you overcome negative attitudes about depression and other mental illnesses?

Glossary

antidepressant (an-tye-di-PRESS-uhnt)—a drug used to relieve the symptoms of depression

biochemical (bye-oh-KEM-uh-kuhl)—reactions of chemical substances with a living organism, such as the human body

chronic (KRON-ik)—continuing for a long time; a person with a chronic disease or condition may have it throughout life.

clinical depression (KLIN-ik-uhl di-PRESH-uhn)—a mood disturbance that must be treated medically

diagnose (dye-uhg-NOHSS)—to determine an illness

dysthymia (diss-THY-mee-uh)—a mild but long-lasting form of depression; a person with dysthymia is able to function in daily life but does not enjoy it.

hallucination (huh-loo-suh-NAY-shuhn)—seeing, hearing, or tasting things that are not really there

norepinephrine (nor-ep-uh-NEF-run)—one of the chemicals in the brain that regulates mood

psychiatrist (sye-KYE-uh-trist)—a medical doctor trained to diagnose and treat mental illness

psychologist (sye-KOL-uh-jist)—a person who provides testing and counseling to people with mental and emotional problems

psychotherapy (sye-koh-THER-uh-pee)—a type of treatment for depression conducted through conversation

rapport (ruh-POR)—a feeling of ease and goodwill between people

serotonin (sihr-oh-TOHN-uhn)—one of the chemicals in the brain that regulates mood

suicide (SOO-uh-side)—the intentional killing of oneself

trauma (TRAW-muh)—a severe and painful emotional or physical shock

For More Information

Ayer, Eleanor H. *Everything You Need to Know About Depression.* New York: Rosen, 1997.

Cobain, Bev. *When Nothing Matters Anymore: A Survival Guide for Depressed Teens.* Minneapolis: Free Spirit, 1998.

Klebanoff, Susan, and Ellen Luborsky. *Ups and Downs: How to Beat the Blues and Teen Depression.* New York: Price Stern Sloan, 1999.

Peacock, Judith. *Bipolar Disorder.* Mankato, MN: Capstone Press, 2000.

Stewart, Gail B. *Teens and Depression.* San Diego: Lucent, 1998.

Useful Addresses and Internet Sites

American Psychiatric Association
1400 K Street Northwest
Suite 501
Washington, DC 20005
www.psych.org

American Association of Suicidology
4201 Connecticut Avenue Northwest
Suite 408
Washington, DC 20008
www.suicidology.org

Canadian Mental Health Association
2160 Yonge Street, 3rd Floor
Toronto, ON M4S 2Z3
CANADA
www.cmha.ca

National Alliance for the Mentally Ill
200 North Glebe Road, Suite 1015
Arlington, VA 22203-3754
1-800-950-6264 (NAMI Helpline)
www.nami.org

National Depressive and Manic-Depressive
Association
730 North Franklin Street
Suite 501
Chicago, IL 60610
1-800-82-NDMDA (800-826-3632)
www.ndmda.org

National Mental Health Association
1021 Prince Street
Alexandria, VA 22314-2971
1-800-969-NMHA (800-969-6642)
www.nmha.org

Depression.com
www.depression.com
Information on many aspects of depression

Suicide Awareness\Voices of Education
(SA\VE)
www.save.org
Information on suicide and links to sites with
further information

DEPRESSION/Awareness, Recognition, and
Treatment Program (D/ART)
1-800-421-4211

Index

acupuncture, 49, 50
alcohol, 10, 19, 25, 34, 36, 40, 45, 46,
        49
alternative therapies, 45, 49–51
anaclitic depression, 9
anger, 17, 25–26, 28, 48, 54, 55, 58
antidepressants, 43–47
    side effects from, 45
attention deficit hyperactivity disorder
        (ADHD), 19

biofeedback, 49, 50
bipolar disorder, 15, 20
brain chemicals, 8, 44, 49

cancer, 6, 12, 18, 23, 35, 57
clinical depression. *See* depression
coaches, 26, 27
communication, 26–30, 59
co-occurring illnesses, 15, 18–19
cost of treatment, 39–41, 46, 59
counselors, 26, 28, 29, 30, 34, 41, 43,
        47
crisis hot lines, 29, 30
crying, 5, 16, 24, 27, 47

death of a loved one, 9. *See also*
        suicide
depression
    causes of, 8–10
    definitions of, 6, 15, 16, 20
    diagnosing, 33–41
    and eating patterns, 7, 24
    effects of, 7, 21
    and females, 10, 15, 17, 19, 20
    getting help for, 23–31, 37
    and males, 10, 15, 17, 18, 20, 25
    symptoms of, 23–26, 38

treatment of, 43–51
types of, 15–21
who gets it, 9, 10–11, 16, 17, 20
diabetes, 9, 18, 35
divorce, 9, 12, 29
drugs, 10, 12, 19, 25, 29, 34, 36, 40,
        41, 43–46, 49. *See also*
        antidepressants
dysthymia, 15, 20–21

eating disorders, 19
emotional shocks, 9
energy, 7, 24, 27, 35, 49, 56
epilepsy, 9, 10
episodic, 15, 16

family, 8, 12, 26, 35–36, 38
    therapy, 48, 55
feeling
    alone, 6, 9, 10, 30, 58
    anxious, 9, 11, 19, 24
    ashamed, 12–13, 38, 39
    empty, 6, 24
    helpless, 6, 24, 28, 55
    hopeless, 7, 24, 37, 39
    sad, 5, 6, 9, 10, 16, 24, 25, 37
    withdrawn, 25, 27
    worried, 5, 7, 9, 11, 47
    worthless, 7, 24
females, 10, 15, 17, 19, 20

grief, 9
group therapy, 48

hallucinations, 16
heart disease, 6, 12, 18, 23, 57
help for depression, 23–31, 37
herbal remedies, 45, 49, 51